The Old Farmer's Almanac
ENGAGEMENT
CALENDAR 2016

Begin the new year square with every man.

–Robert B. Thomas, founder of
The Old Farmer's Almanac (1766–1846)

For appointments, notes, and reminders

Writers: Sarah Perreault, Tim Clark • *Calendar editor:* Heidi Stonehill

Art director: Colleen Quinnell

Contributors: Janice Stillman, Mare-Anne Jarvela, Jack Burnett, Sarah Drory, Catherine Boeckmann

Production assistance: Janet Grant, Rachel Kipka, Jennifer Freeman

Astronomical events are given in Eastern Time.

Cover art: Waterlilies, by Philip Craig

About the cover artist:

Philip Craig lives in Ontario with his wife, Diane. He enjoys painting landscapes, still life, and people engaged in everyday activities, such as sharing a conversation with friends. Incorporating the beauty of color, light, and richly expressive brushwork, Craig's work evokes an element of connection, creating a desire to live within the scene portrayed. His paintings have been purchased by collectors in Canada, the United States, England, and elsewhere and donated by the artist in support of select causes and institutions.

If you find this calendar, please return it to:

Name _____

Address _____

Home _____ Work _____ Cell _____

Copyright © 2015 by Yankee Publishing Incorporated

The Old Farmer's Almanac, P.O. Box 520, Dublin, New Hampshire 03444

Publisher: Sherin Pierce

To order more copies of The Old Farmer's Almanac Engagement Calendar, call 800-ALMANAC or visit our Web site at Almanac.com/Shop.

For wholesale information, contact Stacey Korpi at 800-895-9265, ext. 160.

Printed in U.S.A.

ISBN: 978-1-57198-681-8

2016

bold = *U.S. and/or Canadian national holidays*

JANUARY

S	M	T	W	T	F	S
					1	2
3	4	5	6	7	8	9
10	11	12	13	14	15	16
17	**18**	19	20	21	22	23
24	25	26	27	28	29	30
31						

FEBRUARY

S	M	T	W	T	F	S
	1	2	3	4	5	6
7	8	9	10	11	12	13
14	**15**	16	17	18	19	20
21	22	23	24	25	26	27
28	29					

MARCH

S	M	T	W	T	F	S
		1	2	3	4	5
6	7	8	9	10	11	12
13	14	15	16	17	18	19
20	21	22	23	24	**25**	26
27	**28**	29	30	31		

APRIL

S	M	T	W	T	F	S
					1	2
3	4	5	6	7	8	9
10	11	12	13	14	15	16
17	18	19	20	21	22	23
24	25	26	27	28	29	30

MAY

S	M	T	W	T	F	S
1	2	3	4	5	6	7
8	9	10	11	12	13	14
15	16	17	18	19	20	21
22	**23**	24	25	26	27	28
29	**30**	31				

JUNE

S	M	T	W	T	F	S
			1	2	3	4
5	6	7	8	9	10	11
12	13	14	15	16	17	18
19	20	21	22	23	24	25
26	27	28	29	30		

JULY

S	M	T	W	T	F	S
					1	2
3	**4**	5	6	7	8	9
10	11	12	13	14	15	16
17	18	19	20	21	22	23
24	25	26	27	28	29	30
31						

AUGUST

S	M	T	W	T	F	S
	1	2	3	4	5	6
7	8	9	10	11	12	13
14	15	16	17	18	19	20
21	22	23	24	25	26	27
28	29	30	31			

SEPTEMBER

S	M	T	W	T	F	S
				1	2	3
4	**5**	6	7	8	9	10
11	12	13	14	15	16	17
18	19	20	21	22	23	24
25	26	27	28	29	30	

OCTOBER

S	M	T	W	T	F	S
						1
2	3	4	5	6	7	8
9	**10**	11	12	13	14	15
16	17	18	19	20	21	22
23	24	25	26	27	28	29
30	31					

NOVEMBER

S	M	T	W	T	F	S
		1	2	3	4	5
6	7	8	9	10	**11**	12
13	14	15	16	17	18	19
20	21	22	23	**24**	25	26
27	28	29	30			

DECEMBER

S	M	T	W	T	F	S
				1	2	3
4	5	6	7	8	9	10
11	12	13	14	15	16	17
18	19	20	21	22	23	24
25	**26**	27	28	29	30	31

Look ahead with the 2017/2018 Advance Planners at the back of this calendar.

Shakespeare's Seasons

Here feel we but the penalty of Adam,

The seasons' difference, as the icy fang

And churlish chiding of the winter's wind,

Which, when it bites and blows upon my body,

Even till I shrink with cold, I smile.

–As You Like It

Moon Probe

How did the Moon come to be?

According to the leading theory, an object the size of Mars crashed into young Earth, still in a molten form, splashing sufficient material into orbit to create our Moon. This occurred shortly after the solar system began forming, about 4.5 billion years ago.

FULL WOLF MOON
January 23

Calendar Oddities

Distaff Day: January 7

The first day after Epiphany was the day when women were expected to return to their spinning following the Christmas holiday. A distaff is a staff that women used for holding the flax or wool in spinning (thus the term "distaff" refers to women's work or the maternal side of a family). The equivalent for men was Plough Monday, the first Monday after Epiphany, when men returned to their plowing.

The month of January is like a gentleman— as he begins, so he goes on.

125 Years Ago

January 1891

Live within your income, but do not be so miserly as to refuse to buy John a sled or Jane a doll, even if you have to cut short your ration of tobacco to do it.

–The Old Farmer's Almanac

Folklore from Our Ancestors

How to Cure the Common Cold

- Swallow a spider.
- Cook onions, place in a muslin bag, and wear around the neck.
- Roll orange peels tightly and stuff them up the nostrils.
- Stand on your head underwater.
- Walk with the chin slightly above the horizontal, as if looking at the top of the hat of a man walking in front of you.

December 2015 ❧ January 2016

28 *Monday*

To avoid tough
cookies, do not
overmix the dough.

29 *Tuesday*

Are you chionophobic?
Then you have
a fear of snow.

30 *Wednesday*

It is good practice
to keep at least the last
6 years of tax returns.

31 *Thursday*

May you have warmth in
your igloo, oil in your lamp,
and peace in your heart.
—Inuit proverb

DECEMBER • 2015							JANUARY • 2016						
S	M	T	W	T	F	S	S	M	T	W	T	F	S
		1	2	3	4	5						1	2
6	7	8	9	10	11	12	3	4	5	6	7	8	9
13	14	15	16	17	18	19	10	11	12	13	14	15	16
20	21	22	23	24	25	26	17	18	19	20	21	22	23
27	28	29	30	31			24	25	26	27	28	29	30
							31						

New Year's Day

*Another fresh new
year is here . . .
Another year to live!
To banish worry,
doubt, and fear,
To love and laugh
and give!*

–William Arthur Ward,
American writer (1921–94)

Friday

1

LAST QUARTER

Saturday

2

The first 3 days of
January rule the
coming 3 months.

Carl's B.D. 58 yrs. young!

Sunday

3

REMINDERS

....
....
....
....
....
....

January

4 *Monday*

Hang stale doughnuts and bagels on trees for the woodpeckers.

5 *Tuesday*

Dr. Skullemeis office
Grossnickle's sent my prescription
Dropped my glasses off w/frames

What good fathers and mothers instinctively feel like doing for their babies is the best after all.

–Benjamin Spock,
American physician (1903–98)

6 *Wednesday*

Epiphany

If your foot itches, you will tread strange ground.

7 *Thursday*

Banana is an Arabic word that means "finger."

JANUARY • 2016

S	M	T	W	T	F	S
					1	2
3	4	5	6	7	8	9
10	11	12	13	14	15	16
17	18	19	20	21	22	23
24	25	26	27	28	29	30
31						

FEBRUARY • 2016

S	M	T	W	T	F	S
	1	2	3	4	5	6
7	8	9	10	11	12	13
14	15	16	17	18	19	20
21	22	23	24	25	26	27
28	29					

Friday

8

Today is lucky for
those born under the sign
of Capricorn.

Saturday

9

NEW MOON

Sunday

10

If January calends be
summerly gay,
It will be winterly weather
till the calends of May.

REMINDERS

....

....

....

....

....

....

Complement this calendar with daily weather and Almanac wit and wisdom at Almanac.com.

January

11 Monday

On this day in 1980, Chinook winds warmed an Arctic air mass over Great Falls, Montana, raising the temperature from –32°F to 15°F in 7 minutes.

12 Tuesday

A good head and a good heart are always a formidable combination.

–Nelson Mandela, South African statesman (1918–2013)

13 Wednesday

Save chopsticks from take-out restaurants. They make great plant stakes.

14 Thursday

Picked up glasses - really good! Oops! Seeing double - Left Lens not flush w/ frame

In the language of fruit and vegetables, potato means benevolence.

JANUARY • 2016

S M T W T F S

          1 2
3 4 5 6 7 8 9
10 11 12 13 14 15 16
17 18 19 20 21 22 23
24 25 26 27 28 29 30
31

FEBRUARY • 2016

S M T W T F S

1 2 3 4 5 6
7 8 9 10 11 12 13
14 15 16 17 18 19 20
21 22 23 24 25 26 27
28 29

Friday

15

Walking a mile
through 6 inches of
snow is the same as
walking 2 miles
on bare ground.

Saturday

16

FIRST QUARTER

Benjamin Franklin's
Birthday

*Remember . . . to leave
unsaid the wrong
thing at the tempting
moment.*

–Benjamin Franklin,
American statesman (1706–90)

Sunday

17

Darrel's B. D. 56 yrs. Young
Catherine's B. D.
2-4 @ Mad Anthony's for Jace's B. D.
2 yrs. old 1/18/2014

R E M I N D E R S

....
....
....
....
....
....

January

18 Monday

19 Tuesday

Tina's B.D.

20 Wednesday

21 Thursday

JANUARY • 2016
S M T W T F S
1 2
3 4 5 6 7 8 9
10 11 12 13 14 15 16
17 18 19 20 21 22 23
24 25 26 27 28 29 30
31

FEBRUARY • 2016
S M T W T F S
1 2 3 4 5 6
7 8 9 10 11 12 13
14 15 16 17 18 19 20
21 22 23 24 25 26 27
28 29

St. Vincent

Friday 22

If the Sun shines
on St. Vincent's day,
a fine crop of grapes
may be expected.

Saturday 23

FULL WOLF MOON

Farm Funnies

Sunday 24

Q: Why did the cow
cross the road?

A: To get to the
udder side.

REMINDERS

....
....
....
....
....
....

Complement this calendar with daily weather and Almanac wit and wisdom at Almanac.com.

January

25 Monday
Heather's B. D.

For luck, keep a coin
in your pocket from the year
of your birth.

26 Tuesday

*Nobody will believe in
you unless you
believe in yourself.*
–Liberace, American pianist
(1919–87)

27 Wednesday

Handwriting with
small, irregular spaces
shows that you are
chatty and outgoing.

28 Thursday

When doubling a
recipe, add the
original amount of salt
and then taste before
adding more.

JANUARY • 2016

S	M	T	W	T	F	S
					1	2
3	4	5	6	7	8	9
10	11	12	13	14	15	16
17	18	19	20	21	22	23
24	25	26	27	28	29	30
31						

FEBRUARY • 2016

S	M	T	W	T	F	S
1	2	3	4	5	6	
7	8	9	10	11	12	13
14	15	16	17	18	19	20
21	22	23	24	25	26	27
28	29					

Friday **29**

Knife falls, gentleman calls.
Fork falls, lady calls.
Spoon falls, baby squalls.

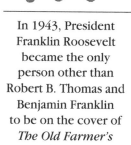

Saturday **30**

In 1943, President Franklin Roosevelt became the only person other than Robert B. Thomas and Benjamin Franklin to be on the cover of *The Old Farmer's Almanac.*

Sunday **31**

LAST QUARTER

REMINDERS

....
....
....
....
....
....

Complement this calendar with daily weather and Almanac wit and wisdom at Almanac.com.

Shakespeare's Seasons

Crabbed age and youth can not live together:

Youth is full of pleasance, age is full of care;

Youth like summer morn, age like winter weather;

Youth like summer brave, age like winter bare.

—The Passionate Pilgrim

Moon Probe

Does Earth have more than one moon?

No, but in 1986, astronomers found a 3-mile-wide asteroid that they called 3753 Cruithne. It is co-orbital with Earth, revolving around the Sun in company with our planet. It never goes completely around Earth and often takes long side trips (inside the orbit of Mercury and outside the orbit of Mars!) before returning.

FULL SNOW MOON
February 22

Calendar Oddities

Candlemas: February 2

Celebrated 40 days after Christmas, this Christian observance is named for the traditional blessing of candles that signify the light of God. Falling midway between the winter solstice and the spring equinox, it also celebrates the lengthening of days. North America's Groundhog Day, when sunny weather is reputed to foretell 6 more weeks of winter, developed in part from Candlemas. New England farmers traditionally believed that you still need "half your wood and half your hay" on Candlemas to get through the winter.

St. Matthias [Feb. 24] breaks the ice; if he finds none, he makes it.

125 Years Ago

February 1891

The lazy and shiftless farmer never thinks of repairing an implement until he is ready to use it, but the industrious and wide-awake farmer does everything he can in the winter to prevent any delay when the busy season comes.

—The Old Farmer's Almanac

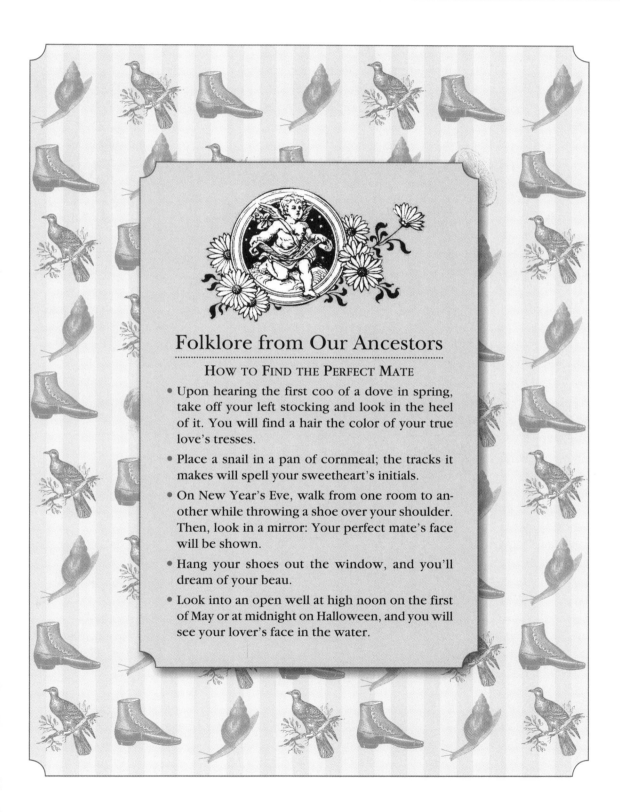

Folklore from Our Ancestors

HOW TO FIND THE PERFECT MATE

- Upon hearing the first coo of a dove in spring, take off your left stocking and look in the heel of it. You will find a hair the color of your true love's tresses.

- Place a snail in a pan of cornmeal; the tracks it makes will spell your sweetheart's initials.

- On New Year's Eve, walk from one room to another while throwing a shoe over your shoulder. Then, look in a mirror: Your perfect mate's face will be shown.

- Hang your shoes out the window, and you'll dream of your beau.

- Look into an open well at high noon on the first of May or at midnight on Halloween, and you will see your lover's face in the water.

February

1 Monday

2 Tuesday

Ground Hog didn't see his Shadow Early Spring !!! Hurry, Hurry

Candlemas

Groundhog Day

At Candlemas, Cold comes to us.

3 Wednesday

fun day @ Sac.

Run out of brass polish? Substitute Worcestershire sauce, ketchup, or toothpaste.

4 Thursday

The name "chicken pox" may have come from the Old English term "gican pox," which means itchy pox.

FEBRUARY • 2016

S M T W T F S
   1 2 3 4 5 6
7 8 9 10 11 12 13
14 15 16 17 18 19 20
21 22 23 24 25 26 27
28 29

MARCH • 2016

S M T W T F S
      1 2 3 4 5
6 7 8 9 10 11 12
13 14 15 16 17 18 19
20 21 22 23 24 25 26
27 28 29 30 31

Pin bay leaves to your pillow to dream of your beloved.

Friday

5

Early pairs of cowboy boots were straight— neither left- nor right-footed.

gave Roger his Card/ B. D.

Saturday

6

No living man All things can.
—*English proverb*

June May needed a Vase for her flowers - I fixed an arrangement for her - My vase - her flowers

Sunday

7

Super Bowl Sunday   Panthers vs Bronco's

REMINDERS

....
....
....
....
....
....

February

8 Monday

NEW MOON

Family Day (B.C.)

9 Tuesday

Mardi Gras (Ala., La.)

To remove a splinter
from your skin,
apply white glue.
Allow the glue to dry
and then peel it off—
the splinter will
come out with it.

10 Wednesday *fun day @ Sac.*

Ash Wednesday

*February brings
the rain,
Thaws the frozen
lake again.*

–Sara Coleridge, English poet
(1802–52)

11 Thursday

Today is lucky for
those born under the sign
of Aquarius.

FEBRUARY • 2016

S	M	T	W	T	F	S
	1	2	3	4	5	6
7	8	9	10	11	12	13
14	15	16	17	18	19	20
21	22	23	24	25	26	27
28	29					

MARCH • 2016

S	M	T	W	T	F	S
		1	2	3	4	5
6	7	8	9	10	11	12
13	14	15	16	17	18	19
20	21	22	23	24	25	26
27	28	29	30	31		

12 — Friday

Abraham Lincoln's Birthday

The Lincoln Memorial Garden in Springfield, Illinois, contains only plants native to Kentucky, Indiana, and Illinois—where the president lived.

Mom's B.D.
Brunch @ 11:00 a.m. Rt. Lizgi's
Men fixed Breakfast
Scrambled eggs, Sausage, Biscuits
Bacon, French Toast, Coffee, O.J.
Sausage, egg Biscuit

13 — Saturday

In the language of fruit and vegetables, pear means affection.

5:30. Sat nite Supper RTigi's
Chix Wings Sour cr., Salsa,
mild Mex Sauce, relish tray &
Spaghetti Salad coffee
set up – dishes Cleaned and everything
back together as was

14 — Sunday

Valentine's Day

Falling in love is like falling down stairs: We never can tell exactly how the thing was done.

–Josh Billings, American humorist
(1818–85)

2:00 – 4:00 WOW Lunch
@ Presbyterian Church – Vonnie
Huffer was a guest + joining

REMINDERS

....
....
....
....
....
....

February

15
Monday   Dad's B. D.

FIRST QUARTER

Washington's Birthday
(observed)

Family Day (Alta., Ont., Sask.)

16
Tuesday 9:30 Exercise w/ Bands

To re-invigorate
houseplants,
remove the top
¼ inch of soil
and top-dress
with fresh
potting soil.

17
Wednesday ~~Exercise~~ Meeting going to form
for Residence of Retired Sizer's
march 24th

*If you can't convince
them, confuse them.*
–Harry S. Truman,
33rd U.S. president (1884–1972)

1:00 Bingo
2:00 B. D. Party for Feb.'s   Vonnie put
Notice together

18
Thursday
10:00 Meeting w/ Julie

To whip cream
more easily, add a
pinch of salt.

FEBRUARY • 2016	MARCH • 2016
S M T W T F S	S M T W T F S
1 2 3 4 5 6	1 2 3 4 5
7 8 9 10 11 12 13	6 7 8 9 10 11 12
14 15 16 17 18 19 20	13 14 15 16 17 18 19
21 22 23 24 25 26 27	20 21 22 23 24 25 26
28 29	27 28 29 30 31

Friday **19**

It is considered unlucky to marry on your birthday.

8:00 a.m. Baked Breakfast rolls for Coffee

3:00 p.m. Cards for Terra / Miller's

Saturday **20**

The most serious charge that can be brought against New England is not Puritanism but February.

–Joseph Wood Krutch, American naturalist (1893–1970)

Left @ 10:30 w/ Fern + Carl Road trip South to R.V World @ Fisher's - Ate at Logan's Road House and stopped @ D.Q in Wabash

Sunday **21**

Farm Funnies

Q: What do you call the horse that lives next door?

A: Your neigh-bor.

Rested --

REMINDERS

....
....
....
....
....
....

February

22 Monday

Labs   Beyer Building
9:10 A.m
Had Blood Work this a. m.
Fern's Birthday - Breakfast @ Richards

FULL SNOW MOON

23 Tuesday

24 Wednesday

Handwriting that
slants up the
page shows that
you are optimistic
and content.

25 Thursday

FEBRUARY • 2016							MARCH • 2016					
S	M	T	W	T	F	S	S	M	T	W	T	F	S
	1	2	3	4	5	6			1	2	3	4	5
7	8	9	10	11	12	13	6	7	8	9	10	11	12
14	15	16	17	18	19	20	13	14	15	16	17	18	19
21	22	23	24	25	26	27	20	21	22	23	24	25	26
28	29						27	28	29	30	31		

Friday 26

Heritage Day (Y.T.)

When the cat in February
lies in the sun, she
will again creep behind the
stove in March.

Saturday 27

*Honey mixed with
pulverized pure
charcoal is said to
be excellent to cleanse
the teeth and make
them white.*

–Lydia Maria Child,
American Frugal Housewife, 1832

Sunday 28

To grow your own
filling for Easter
baskets, start grass
seeds on a sponge in
a dish of water.

REMINDERS

....
....
....
....
....
....

Complement this calendar with daily weather and Almanac wit and wisdom at Almanac.com.

29 *Monday*

Dr's appointment
9:20

Leap Day

Leap Day was once
known as Ladies' Day,
as it was the one
day when it was
acceptable for women
to propose to men.

---

1 *Tuesday*

LAST QUARTER

Town Meeting Day (Vt.)

---

2 *Wednesday*

Texas Independence Day

Austin, Texas, is
home to North
America's largest
urban bat colony.

---

3 *Thursday*

*Surely as cometh
the Winter,
I know there are
Spring violets
under the snow.*

–R. H. Newell, American poet
(1836–1901)

FEBRUARY • 2016							MARCH • 2016						
S	M	T	W	T	F	S	S	M	T	W	T	F	S
	1	2	3	4	5	6			1	2	3	4	5
7	8	9	10	11	12	13	6	7	8	9	10	11	12
14	15	16	17	18	19	20	13	14	15	16	17	18	19
21	22	23	24	25	26	27	20	21	22	23	24	25	26
28	29						27	28	29	30	31		

Friday 4

If you sneeze while eating at a table, you will have a new friend before the next meal.

Saturday 5

In the language of fruit and vegetables, pineapple says, "You are perfect."

Sunday 6

I can't go back to yesterday because I was a different person then.

–Lewis Carroll, English writer (1832–98)

REMINDERS

....
....
....
....
....
....

Shakespeare's Seasons

The spring, the summer,

The childing [fruitful] *autumn, angry winter change*

Their wonted liveries; and the mazèd world

By their increase, now knows not which is which.

–A Midsummer Night's Dream

Moon Probe

What shape is the Moon?

Although it looks round to observers on Earth, the Moon is actually egg-shape. One theory suggests that when the Moon was formed, it had a smaller companion that eventually fell into it. The impact coated the far side with enough debris to create a bulge.

FULL WORM MOON
March 23

Calendar Oddities

Evacuation Day: March 17

This holiday is observed only in Suffolk County, Massachusetts. Although it officially commemorates the evacuation of British troops from Boston on this date in 1776, the connection to St. Patrick's Day is more than coincidental. When George Washington secretly moved artillery to Dorchester Heights, where the guns would threaten the British fleet, the password for the night march was "Boston" and the countersign was "St. Patrick." When Suffolk County formally recognized Evacuation Day in 1941, the proclamation was signed in both black and green ink.

March, many weathers.

125 Years Ago

March 1891

Few things that cost so little add so much to the happiness of the members of the household as a well-kept flower garden. Every farmer should teach his children to read intelligently the wonderful book of nature.

–The Old Farmer's Almanac

Folklore from Our Ancestors

HOW TO KEEP BABIES HEALTHY

- Burn the first dirty diaper, and the baby will have no stomachaches.
- If the baby is croupy, mix a lock of its hair with the mortar in a new house.
- To prevent croup, feed the baby jaybird soup.
- Lay a grunting baby in the pigpen to make him stop.
- After a baby has eaten, let a puppy lick its face to discourage illness.

March

7 *Monday*

To cure hiccups, have someone drop a cold key down your back.

8 *Tuesday*

NEW MOON

9 *Wednesday*

The bigfin squid has elbows.

10 *Thursday*

As long as the Sun shines, one does not ask for the Moon.
—Russian proverb

MARCH • 2016	APRIL • 2016
S M T W T F S	S M T W T F S
1 2 3 4 5	1 2
6 7 8 9 10 11 12	3 4 5 6 7 8 9
13 14 15 16 17 18 19	10 11 12 13 14 15 16
20 21 22 23 24 25 26	17 18 19 20 21 22 23
27 28 29 30 31	24 25 26 27 28 29 30

Friday **11**

*March brings breezes
loud and shrill,
Stirs the dancing
daffodil.*

–Sara Coleridge,
English poet (1802–52)

*Not Blooming yet!
Buds on tree out
front getting Redder & bigger*

Saturday **12**

Today is lucky for
those born under the sign
of Pisces.

Sunday **13**

Daylight Saving Time begins
at 2:00 A.M.

Lose an hour in the
morning and you'll be all
day hunting for it.

*New Time
Lazy Day*

REMINDERS

....
....
....
....
....
....

March

14 Monday

Funky Day,
Bad depression!

missed coloring

15 Tuesday

New Lantus   *Exercise*
* '' Humalog*   *9:30*

2:00 B.D. Party & Bingo
Miller's

FIRST QUARTER

16 Wednesday

17 Thursday

St Patty's Day
Wearing the Green

MARCH • 2016

S	M	T	W	T	F	S
		1	2	3	4	5
6	7	8	9	10	11	12
13	14	15	16	17	18	19
20	21	22	23	24	25	26
27	28	29	30	31		

APRIL • 2016

S	M	T	W	T	F	S
					1	2
3	4	5	6	7	8	9
10	11	12	13	14	15	16
17	18	19	20	21	22	23
24	25	26	27	28	29	30

Friday 18

The Sun makes up 99.86% of our solar system's mass.

Saturday 19

Store girls' barrettes and other hair accessories in a large fishbowl.

Sunday 20

Palm Sunday

Sunday of Orthodoxy

Vernal Equinox

Rain in the spring is as precious as oil.
—*Chinese proverb*

REMINDERS

....
....
....
....
....
....

March

21 *Monday*

Finding a pair of gloves foreshadows a successful business week.

22 *Tuesday*

A puffy capital P in handwriting shows that you feel vulnerable.

23 *Wednesday*

FULL WORM MOON

24 *Thursday*

Cheerily the chickadee Singeth to me on fence and tree.

–John Townsend Trowbridge, American author (1827–1916)

MARCH • 2016	APRIL • 2016
S M T W T F S	S M T W T F S
1 2 3 4 5	1 2
6 7 8 9 10 11 12	3 4 5 6 7 8 9
13 14 15 16 17 18 19	10 11 12 13 14 15 16
20 21 22 23 24 25 26	17 18 19 20 21 22 23
27 28 29 30 31	24 25 26 27 28 29 30

Friday 25

Good Friday

Bread baked on Good Friday
will not go moldy.

Farm Funnies

Saturday 26

Q: What do you call a
sleeping bull?

A: A bull-dozer.

Easter

Sunday 27

Seventy-six percent of
people eat the ears of a
chocolate bunny first.

REMINDERS

....
....
....
....
....
....

March ✣ April

28 *Monday*

Save empty milk jugs
to make tomato
hotcaps (mini
greenhouses).

29 *Tuesday*

Leave your shoes
in the shape of a
"T" overnight to guard
against nightmares.

30 *Wednesday*

*A man all wrapped
up in himself makes a
small parcel.*

–John Ruskin, English art critic
(1819–1900)

31 *Thursday*

LAST QUARTER

MARCH • 2016

S	M	T	W	T	F	S
		1	2	3	4	5
6	7	8	9	10	11	12
13	14	15	16	17	18	19
20	21	22	23	24	25	26
27	28	29	30	31		

APRIL • 2016

S	M	T	W	T	F	S
					1	2
3	4	5	6	7	8	9
10	11	12	13	14	15	16
17	18	19	20	21	22	23
24	25	26	27	28	29	30

All Fools' Day

Friday 1

If your nose itches,
you may kiss a fool in
the near future.

Pascua Florida Day

Saturday 2

Everglades National
Park contains the
slowest-moving river in
the world.

Sunday 3

From word to deed
is a great space.

REMINDERS

....
....
....
....
....
....

Shakespeare's Seasons

From you have I been absent in the spring,

When proud pied April, dressed in all his trim,

Hath put a spirit of youth in every thing.

—Sonnet 98

Moon Probe

What happened to the rocks that the Apollo astronauts brought back from the Moon?

Most of the 842 pounds of Moon rocks are still in the hands of NASA, independent scientists who received samples to study, and 135 states and 270 foreign countries that were given rocks as gifts. But, more than 500 samples have gone missing.

FULL PINK MOON
April 22

Calendar Oddities

Shakespeare's Birthday: April 23

Although there is no official record of the date of the Bard's birth, church records say that he was baptized on April 26, 1564, and scholars believe that the sacrament was usually administered 3 days after birth.

In April, each drop counts for a thousand.

125 Years Ago

April 1891

Encourage the boys to get up a [maple] sugar party. If the boys are to be kept on the farm, and the girls made contented and happy, they must be encouraged to hold frequent social gatherings.

—The Old Farmer's Almanac

Folklore from Our Ancestors

HOW TO GET RICH WITHOUT WORKING

- Always cut your fingernails on Tuesday.
- Touch the money in your pocket whenever you hear a whippoorwill.
- Look at the new Moon with money in your hands.
- When you see a shooting star, say "Money, money, money!" before it disappears.
- Spit on the first money that you receive each day.

April

4 *Monday*

Pour equal parts vinegar and scouring cleanser on burned food in the bottom of a nonreactive cooking pan and let it set overnight. It will wash away easily in the morning.

5 *Tuesday*

Today is lucky for those born under the sign of Aries.

6 *Wednesday*

In the language of fruit and vegetables, olive means peace.

7 *Thursday*

NEW MOON

APRIL • 2016							MAY • 2016						
S	M	T	W	T	F	S	S	M	T	W	T	F	S
					1	2	1	2	3	4	5	6	7
3	4	5	6	7	8	9	8	9	10	11	12	13	14
10	11	12	13	14	15	16	15	16	17	18	19	20	21
17	18	19	20	21	22	23	22	23	24	25	26	27	28
24	25	26	27	28	29	30	29	30	31				

Friday **8**

*April brings the
primrose sweet,
Scatters daisies
at our feet.*

–Sara Coleridge, English poet
(1802–52)

Saturday **9**

A dream of coconuts
heralds the arrival of an
unexpected gift.

Sunday **10**

On this day in
1872, the first Arbor
Day was celebrated
in Nebraska.

REMINDERS

....
....
....
....
....
....

April

11 Monday

It is better to deserve without receiving than to receive without deserving.

–Robert Green Ingersoll, American lawyer (1833–99)

12 Tuesday

When putting your belongings in a storage unit, leave a center aisle to access items easily.

13 Wednesday

FIRST QUARTER

Thomas Jefferson's Birthday

14 Thursday

When black snails on the road you see, Then on the morrow rain will be.

APRIL • 2016

S	M	T	W	T	F	S
					1	2
3	4	5	6	7	8	9
10	11	12	13	14	15	16
17	18	19	20	21	22	23
24	25	26	27	28	29	30

MAY • 2016

S	M	T	W	T	F	S
1	2	3	4	5	6	7
8	9	10	11	12	13	14
15	16	17	18	19	20	21
22	23	24	25	26	27	28
29	30	31				

Friday **15**

The thing you have to be prepared for is that other people don't always dream your dream.

–Linda Ronstadt, American singer (b. 1946)

Saturday **16**

A pair of crows seen at a wedding brings good luck to the bride and groom.

Sunday **17**

Don't exceed the feed limit.

–Jack LaLanne, American fitness expert (1914–2011)

REMINDERS

....

April

18 Monday

Wide handwriting
shows that you are a
self-oriented person.

19 Tuesday

Break an egg,
Break your leg;
Break three,
Woe to thee;
Break two,
Your love's true.

20 Wednesday

One Brazil nut a day
gives you the
recommended dietary
allowance (RDA) of
selenium, an
antioxidant mineral.

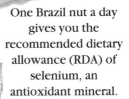

21 Thursday

*When I was born,
I was so surprised
that I didn't talk for a
year and a half.*

–Gracie Allen,
American comedienne (1902–64)

APRIL • 2016							MAY • 2016						
S	M	T	W	T	F	S	S	M	T	W	T	F	S
					1	2	1	2	3	4	5	6	7
3	4	5	6	7	8	9	8	9	10	11	12	13	14
10	11	12	13	14	15	16	15	16	17	18	19	20	21
17	18	19	20	21	22	23	22	23	24	25	26	27	28
24	25	26	27	28	29	30	29	30	31				

Friday 22

FULL PINK MOON

Passover begins at sundown

Earth Day

Saturday 23

St. George's Day,
traditional (N.L.)

April showers,
Cool and pouring—
Keep it up,
It's getting boring.
–The Old Farmer's Almanac, 1983

Sunday 24

Birthday of Robert
B. Thomas, founder
of *The Old Farmer's*
Almanac

REMINDERS

....
....
....
....
....
....

April ❧ May

25 *Monday*

Put an old bookcase in the garage for storing flowerpots, gardening tools, work gloves, sunscreen, and insect repellent.

26 *Tuesday*

The 134-mile-wide Galle Crater on Mars has ridges that form a smiling face, earning it the nickname of "Happy Face" Crater.

27 *Wednesday*

Deter cats by spreading chopped citrus peels around your garden. Repeat biweekly.

28 *Thursday*

Farm Funnies

Q: What is a rabbit's favorite kind of music?

A: Hip-hop.

APRIL • 2016

S	M	T	W	T	F	S
					1	2
3	4	5	6	7	8	9
10	11	12	13	14	15	16
17	18	19	20	21	22	23
24	25	26	27	28	29	30

MAY • 2016

S	M	T	W	T	F	S
1	2	3	4	5	6	7
8	9	10	11	12	13	14
15	16	17	18	19	20	21
22	23	24	25	26	27	28
29	30	31				

Friday 29

LAST QUARTER

National Arbor Day

Saturday 30

*Adopt the pace
of nature: Her secret
is patience.*

–Ralph Waldo Emerson,
American poet (1803–82)

Sunday 1

Orthodox Easter

May Day

Tomorrow is often the
busiest day of the week.

–*Spanish proverb*

REMINDERS

....
....
....
....
....
....

Shakespeare's Seasons

Love, whose month is ever May,

Spied a blossom passing fair

Playing in the wanton air.

—*Love's Labours Lost*

Moon Probe

What is at the center of the Moon?

For centuries, some have believed the Moon to be hollow or an alien spacecraft, but NASA scientists think that the Moon's outer crust and thick underlying mantle surround several core layers: Between the mantle and core is a nearly 300-mile-thick boundary layer of partially molten material. This in turn wraps a molten iron outer core that is about 205 miles thick. At the center is a solid iron inner core about 300 miles in diameter.

FULL FLOWER MOON
May 21

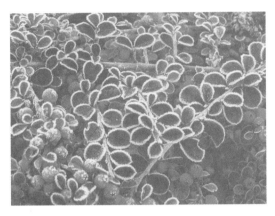

Calendar Oddities

Three Chilly Saints: May 11, 12, 13

The Christian saints Mamertus, Pancras, and Gervais are in part remembered because their feast days are often cold in northern Europe. An old French weather adage translates as "St. Mamertus, St. Pancras, and St. Gervais do not pass without a frost."

In the middle of May comes the tail of the winter.

125 Years Ago

May 1891

Nothing like being in season, especially at planting time. To plant a week too late often means a loss of at least one-third of the crop; and a week late in hoeing doubles the labor of keeping the weeds down.

—The Old Farmer's Almanac

Folklore from Our Ancestors

HOW TO PLANT CROPS

- To make a plant grow, spit into the hole that you have dug for it.

- The best way to ensure that plant slips will thrive is to steal them.

- Never plant anything on the 31st of the month.

- Flax will grow well if you show it your buttocks.

- Peppers should be planted only by a violent-tempered person, a red-haired person, or a person in a bad mood.

May

2 Monday

A cold May is good for corn and hay.

3 Tuesday

Drye roses put to ye nose to smell do comforte the brain.

–Anthony Askham,
A Litle Herball, 1550

4 Wednesday

Remove odors from plastic containers by filling them with crumpled newspaper. Cover and let sit overnight.

5 Thursday

Cinco de Mayo

Today is lucky for those born under the sign of Taurus.

MAY • 2016							JUNE • 2016						
S	M	T	W	T	F	S	S	M	T	W	T	F	S
1	2	3	4	5	6	7				1	2	3	4
8	9	10	11	12	13	14	5	6	7	8	9	10	11
15	16	17	18	19	20	21	12	13	14	15	16	17	18
22	23	24	25	26	27	28	19	20	21	22	23	24	25
29	30	31					26	27	28	29	30		

Friday

6

NEW MOON

To encourage new growth, prune shrubs and trees between the new and full Moons.

Saturday

7

Mother's Day

Truman Day, traditional (Mo.)

God could not be everywhere, and therefore He made mothers.

–Rudyard Kipling, English writer (1865–1936)

Sunday

8

REMINDERS

....
....
....
....
....

May

9 *Monday*

On the way to your wedding, it is good luck to meet a chimney sweep, elephant, or toad.

10 *Tuesday*

The side of a hammer's head is called the cheek.

11 *Wednesday*

If bats fly abroad after sunset, expect fair weather.

12 *Thursday*

May brings flocks of pretty lambs, Skipping by their fleecy dams.

–Sara Coleridge, English poet (1802–52)

MAY • 2016							JUNE • 2016					
S	M	T	W	T	F	S	S	M	T	W	T	F	S
1	2	3	4	5	6	7				1	2	3	4
8	9	10	11	12	13	14	5	6	7	8	9	10	11
15	16	17	18	19	20	21	12	13	14	15	16	17	18
22	23	24	25	26	27	28	19	20	21	22	23	24	25
29	30	31					26	27	28	29	30		

FIRST QUARTER

Friday

13

In the language of
fruit and vegetables,
raspberry means
remorse.

Saturday

14

Whitsunday—Pentecost

A capital "D" with
an open top in
handwriting shows
that you are a
social person.

Sunday

15

REMINDERS

....
....
....
....
....
....

May

16 Monday

*The best fertilizer for
a piece of land is the
footprints of its owner.*

–Lyndon B. Johnson,
36th U.S. president (1908–73)

17 Tuesday

If a young lady accidentally
pricks her finger
while sewing a new dress,
she will be kissed while
wearing the dress.

18 Wednesday

*Just living is not
enough . . . one must
have sunshine,
freedom, and a little
flower.*

–Hans Christian Andersen,
Danish writer (1805–75)

19 Thursday

The total weight
of all ants on Earth
is close to that
of all humans.

	MAY • 2016							JUNE • 2016					
S	M	T	W	T	F	S	S	M	T	W	T	F	S
1	2	3	4	5	6	7				1	2	3	4
8	9	10	11	12	13	14	5	6	7	8	9	10	11
15	16	17	18	19	20	21	12	13	14	15	16	17	18
22	23	24	25	26	27	28	19	20	21	22	23	24	25
29	30	31					26	27	28	29	30		

Friday 20

Many thunderstorms
in May,
And the farmer sings,
"Hey! Hey!"

Saturday 21

FULL FLOWER MOON

Armed Forces Day

Sunday 22

National Maritime Day

High seas come to the sailor
who dreams of horses.

REMINDERS

....
....
....
....
....

Complement this calendar with daily weather and Almanac wit and wisdom at Almanac.com.

May

23 _Monday_

Skating teaches you to do the things you should do before you do the things you want to do.

–Barbara Ann Scott,
Canadian figure skater
(1928–2012)

24 _Tuesday_

A mailbox mounted on a post near the garden provides weatherproof storage for seed packets.

25 _Wednesday_

Give your children too much freedom, and you lose your own.

–Russian proverb

26 _Thursday_

Farm Funnies

Q: What new crop did the farmer plant?

A: Beets me!

MAY • 2016							JUNE • 2016						
S	M	T	W	T	F	S	S	M	T	W	T	F	S
1	2	3	4	5	6	7				1	2	3	4
8	9	10	11	12	13	14	5	6	7	8	9	10	11
15	16	17	18	19	20	21	12	13	14	15	16	17	18
22	23	24	25	26	27	28	19	20	21	22	23	24	25
29	30	31					26	27	28	29	30		

Daylilies are not
lilies; they are
members of the genus
Hemerocallis.

Friday 27

If bees stay at home,
Rain will soon come;
If they fly away,
Fine will be the day.

Saturday 28

LAST QUARTER

Sunday 29

Reminders

....
....
....
....
....
....

May 🌿 June

30 Monday

There are about 900,000 poppy seeds in 1 pound.

31 Tuesday

One should know everything that one says, but not say everything that one knows.

–*The Old Farmer's Almanac*, 1901

1 Wednesday

Rub strong chamomile tea over your skin: It is a natural bug repellent.

2 Thursday

It is lucky to put on an apron inside out.

MAY • 2016	JUNE • 2016
S M T W T F S	S M T W T F S
1 2 3 4 5 6 7	1 2 3 4
8 9 10 11 12 13 14	5 6 7 8 9 10 11
15 16 17 18 19 20 21	12 13 14 15 16 17 18
22 23 24 25 26 27 28	19 20 21 22 23 24 25
29 30 31	26 27 28 29 30

Wedding
"bomboniera," or
packets of sugared
almonds, symbolize
health, happiness,
and fertility.

Friday

3

NEW MOON

Saturday

4

Ramadan begins at sundown

World Environment Day

Air is medicine.

–Lillian Russell, American actress
(1861–1922)

Sunday

5

REMINDERS

....

....

....

....

....

....

Shakespeare's Seasons

He was but as the cuckoo is in June,

Heard, not regarded; seen, but with such eyes

As, sick and blunted with community,

Afford no extraordinary gaze . . .

–Henry IV, Part 1

Moon Probe

How does the full Moon compare in brightness to the Sun?

The Sun, which produces its own light, has a magnitude of about –26.7 (the lower the number, the brighter the object). The full Moon, which is bright only because sunlight bounces off it, has a magnitude of about –12.6. This means that the Sun is about 400,000 times brighter than the full Moon.

FULL STRAWBERRY MOON
June 20

Calendar Oddities

Midsummer Day: June 24

To the farmer, this day is the midpoint of the growing season, halfway between planting and harvest. It is also near (although not on) the summer solstice. The Anglican church considered it a "Quarter Day," one of the four major divisions of the liturgical year. It also marks the feast day of St. John the Baptist. The night before, Midsummer Eve, is an occasion for festivities celebrating fertility. It predates Christianity, and some traditional rites, such as building bonfires, go back to the dawn of civilization.

Never rued the man who got in his fuel [firewood] before St. John [June 24].

125 Years Ago

June 1891

Lazy farmers don't like weeds, yet they grow more of them in their gardens than anyone else. They cultivate just often enough to keep the weeds in good condition.

–The Old Farmer's Almanac

Folklore from Our Ancestors

HOW TO CURE A TOOTHACHE

- The Roman naturalist Pliny recommended eating a mouse twice a month.
- Kiss a donkey.
- Put your right ring finger into your left ear.
- Hold a live frog against the aching cheek.
- Pick your tooth with the nail of the middle toe of an owl.

June

6 *Monday*

Cut ruined nylons into strips and use them as ties to secure plants to garden stakes.

7 *Tuesday*

June brings tulips, lilies, roses, Fills the children's hand with posies.

–Sara Coleridge, English poet (1802–52)

8 *Wednesday*

When cows stray from home, find a granddaddy (daddy longlegs) spider and ask it, "Granddaddy, Granddaddy, where are my cows?" He will point a foot in the right direction.

9 *Thursday*

To make your own insecticidal soap, combine 2 tablespoons of liquid soap with 1 gallon of water.

JUNE • 2016

S	M	T	W	T	F	S
			1	2	3	4
5	6	7	8	9	10	11
12	13	14	15	16	17	18
19	20	21	22	23	24	25
26	27	28	29	30		

JULY • 2016

S	M	T	W	T	F	S
					1	2
3	4	5	6	7	8	9
10	11	12	13	14	15	16
17	18	19	20	21	22	23
24	25	26	27	28	29	30
31						

Friday 10

On this day in 1752, Benjamin Franklin's kite-and-key experiment resulted in his discovery that lightning is electricity.

Saturday 11

King Kamehameha I Day, traditional (Hawaii)

Astronauts once trained for Moon voyages by walking on the hardened lava fields of Mauna Loa, a volcano on Hawaii.

Sunday 12

FIRST QUARTER

REMINDERS

....

....

....

....

....

....

June

13 Monday

Today is lucky for
those born under the sign
of Gemini.

14 Tuesday

Flag Day

To fly a flag at
half-mast, it should
be first raised
completely and then
lowered halfway.

15 Wednesday

*This month's
weather's Jekyll and
Hyde—hottish,
coolish, it can't decide.*
—The Old Farmer's Almanac, 1997

16 Thursday

It is not enough to know
how to ride; You must
also know how to fall.
—Mexican proverb

JUNE • 2016	JULY • 2016
S M T W T F S	S M T W T F S
1 2 3 4	1 2
5 6 7 8 9 10 11	3 4 5 6 7 8 9
12 13 14 15 16 17 18	10 11 12 13 14 15 16
19 20 21 22 23 24 25	17 18 19 20 21 22 23
26 27 28 29 30	24 25 26 27 28 29 30
	31

Friday 17

Bunker Hill Day
(Suffolk Co., Mass.)

"Duck" comes from
the Anglo-Saxon
word *duce,* which
means "diver."

Saturday 18

Small handwriting
shows that you
are reserved and not
overly confident.

Sunday 19

Orthodox Pentecost

Father's Day

Emancipation Day (Tex.)

One father is more than a
hundred schoolmasters.
–English proverb

REMINDERS

....

....

....

....

....

....

June

20 *Monday*

FULL STRAWBERRY MOON

Summer Solstice

West Virginia Day

21 *Tuesday*

National Aboriginal Day
(Canada)

Do not wash
strawberries until you
are ready to eat or
use them. Moisture
will cause the
berries to become
mushy.

22 *Wednesday*

*Holy Toledo—who
invented the mosquito?*
–The Old Farmer's Almanac, 1980

23 *Thursday*

In the language of fruit
and vegetables,
cucumber implies
criticism.

| JUNE • 2016 | | | | | | | JULY • 2016 | | | | | |
S	M	T	W	T	F	S	S	M	T	W	T	F	S
			1	2	3	4						1	2
5	6	7	8	9	10	11	3	4	5	6	7	8	9
12	13	14	15	16	17	18	10	11	12	13	14	15	16
19	20	21	22	23	24	25	17	18	19	20	21	22	23
26	27	28	29	30			24	25	26	27	28	29	30
							31						

Fête Nationale (Qué.)

Friday 24

Words are like bees: They
have honey and a sting.

—German proverb

Farm Funnies

Saturday 25

Q: Why did the
chicken cross the
playground?

A: To get to the
other slide.

*Big doesn't necessarily
mean better.
Sunflowers aren't
better than violets.*

Sunday 26

–Edna Ferber, American writer
(1887–1968)

REMINDERS

....

....

....

....

....

....

June ❧ July

27 *Monday*

LAST QUARTER

Discovery Day, observed
(N.L.)

28 *Tuesday*

*An eye for an eye
ends up making the
whole world blind.*

–Mahatma Gandhi, Indian
spiritual leader (1869–1948)

29 *Wednesday*

Chicken tetrazzini
was named for Italian
opera singer Luisa
Tetrazzini, who
was born on this day
in 1871.

30 *Thursday*

Mackerel sky, mackerel sky,
Never long wet, never long dry.

The Easiest Thing You'll Do All Year!

How would you like to receive next year's elegant Engagement Calendar *PLUS* a FREE copy of our *Everyday Recipes* cookbook *AND* save the hassle of reordering?

Order your 2017 calendar today, and for the first year, we'll send a copy of *The Old Farmer's Almanac Everyday Recipes Cookbook* as our FREE gift to you (a $9.99 value)! **The Old Farmer's Almanac Engagement Calendar** is a stylish and timesaving companion you can count on to manage your daily appointments and activities. This hard-bound desk calendar features space for addresses and phone numbers, weekly reminders, and 2018 and 2019 advance planners! PLUS, you can enjoy Almanac weather proverbs, folklore, fun facts, quotes, and more!

Due to mailing requirements, we regret that we are unable to offer this program outside of the United States.

CALENDAR REORDER FORM

☐ Send me the 2017 Engagement Calendar, plus my FREE gift! (Includes renewal plan.)*

Name_____

Street_____

City_____State_____ Zip_____

☐ Check enclosed   Charge my: ☐ Visa ☐ MasterCard ☐ AmEx ☐ Discover

Acct. No._____Exp._____

Signature_____
required for credit card orders

The Old Farmer's Almanac 2017 Engagement Calendar
Qty. calendars ordered _____
× $19.95 $_____
s&h add $ 5.95
Total enclosed $_____
SKU: 0317CEGB Promo: EGC76EEC

THREE EASY WAYS TO ORDER!

✉ **MAIL this form with payment to: The Old Farmer's Almanac, P.O. Box 450, Mt. Morris, IL 61054**

☎ **PHONE: Call toll-free 1-800-ALMANAC (1-800-256-2622).**

🖱 **ONLINE: Visit Almanac.com/Shop**

*Enter my guaranteed reservation for all future editions of The Old Farmer's Almanac Engagement Calendar at the lowest price available. I will get a BONUS gift every time, just for looking. Next July, I will receive an advance notice of shipment of the 2017 calendar and my BONUS gift. NO OBLIGATION! I may use that card to change my address, change my order, or cancel next year's shipment. I am under no obligation to purchase future calendars and may cancel at any time.

Calendar will ship in September.

EGC76EEC

Name: _____

Address: _____

_____

City/Town: _____ State: _____ Zip: _____

BUSINESS REPLY MAIL
FIRST-CLASS MAIL PERMIT NO. 500 MT. MORRIS IL

POSTAGE WILL BE PAID BY ADDRESSEE

The Old Farmer's Almanac
PO Box 450
Mt. Morris IL 61054-9903

Fold along this line. ▲

After cutting this order form out of the book along the vertical dotted line, fold it in half along the horizontal dotted line. Please be sure to either complete the payment information on the order form or enclose a check. Then tape the envelope closed along the three open edges. DO NOT SEND CASH.

Cut along dotted line. ▶

Use clear tape on all three open sides to seal completely.

JUNE • 2016

S	M	T	W	T	F	S
			1	2	3	4
5	6	7	8	9	10	11
12	13	14	15	16	17	18
19	20	21	22	23	24	25
26	27	28	29	30		

JULY • 2016

S	M	T	W	T	F	S
					1	2
3	4	5	6	7	8	9
10	11	12	13	14	15	16
17	18	19	20	21	22	23
24	25	26	27	28	29	30
31						

Canada Day

Friday

1

Masters in our own house we must be, but our house is the whole of Canada.

–Pierre Trudeau, Canadian prime minister (1919–2000)

Saturday

2

To remove stains from delicate fabrics, dissolve 2 tablespoons of cream of tartar in 1 gallon of hot water. Cool, then soak the stain in the solution.

Sunday

3

It is lucky to set out to sea on a Sunday.

REMINDERS

....
....
....
....
....
....

Shakespeare's Seasons

Sometime too hot the eye of heaven shines,

And often is his gold complexion dimm'd;

And every fair from fair sometime declines,

By chance or nature's changing course untrimm'd.

—Sonnet 18

Moon Probe

Who was first to reach the Moon?

The first vertebrate creatures to circle the Moon were a pair of Russian steppe tortoises. Along with mealworms, wine flies, seeds, and bacteria, they were part of a biological payload in the *Zond 5* spacecraft launched by the Soviet Union on September 15, 1968.

FULL BUCK MOON
July 19

Calendar Oddities

Dog Days begin: July 3

The 40 days beginning now are traditionally the hottest and unhealthiest of the year (in the Northern Hemisphere). They once coincided with the rise of the Dog Star, Sirius, at dawn. The ancients believed that it was the combined heat of Sirius and the Sun that made the summer swelter.

Never trust a July sky.

125 Years Ago

July 1891

At this season of the year, it is a good plan to begin work in the cool of the morning and rest an hour or two at midday when the heat is most oppressive.

—The Old Farmer's Almanac

Folklore from Our Ancestors

How to Cure Insomnia

- Smell your socks after taking them off before bed.
- Lie down in bed so that your head points north.
- Tie the dried root of a peony around your neck.
- Shake the bedclothes 20 times before getting under them.
- Count sheep or count crows circling in the sky.

July

4 Monday

NEW MOON

Independence Day

5 Tuesday

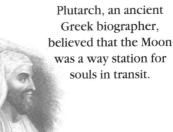

Plutarch, an ancient Greek biographer, believed that the Moon was a way station for souls in transit.

6 Wednesday

For long-lasting blooms, pick flowers in the late afternoon, when the leaves and stems contain the most sugar.

7 Thursday

Hot July brings cooling showers, Apricots and gillyflowers.

–Sara Coleridge, English poet (1802–52)

JULY • 2016							AUGUST • 2016					
S	M	T	W	T	F	S	S	M	T	W	T	F	S
					1	2		1	2	3	4	5	6
3	4	5	6	7	8	9	7	8	9	10	11	12	13
10	11	12	13	14	15	16	14	15	16	17	18	19	20
17	18	19	20	21	22	23	21	22	23	24	25	26	27
24	25	26	27	28	29	30	28	29	30	31			
31													

Friday **8**

In the language of
fruit and vegetables,
peach says,
"You're terrific."

Saturday **9**

Nunavut Day (Canada)

Nunavut means
"our land" in the
Inuktitut language.

Sunday **10**

If an expectant mother
sees a donkey, her child
will grow up to be
well behaved and wise.

REMINDERS

July

11 Monday

FIRST QUARTER

12 Tuesday

Orangemen's Day,
traditional (N.L.)

On this day in 2011,
Neptune completed
its first orbit around
the Sun since its
discovery in 1846.

13 Wednesday

To prevent tough
skins on blueberries,
do not rinse them
before freezing.

14 Thursday

Who is it?
–the last words of Billy the Kid,
outlaw of the American West
(1859–81), on this day in 1881

JULY • 2016

S	M	T	W	T	F	S
					1	2
3	4	5	6	7	8	9
10	11	12	13	14	15	16
17	18	19	20	21	22	23
24	25	26	27	28	29	30
31						

AUGUST • 2016

S	M	T	W	T	F	S
	1	2	3	4	5	6
7	8	9	10	11	12	13
14	15	16	17	18	19	20
21	22	23	24	25	26	27
28	29	30	31			

Friday 15

Tall handwriting
shows that
you crave approval.

Saturday 16

Plant a second crop
of lettuce, radishes,
and spinach to
harvest in the fall.

Sunday 17

*Never lose sight of
the fact that the most
important yardstick
of your success
will be how you
treated other people.*

–Barbara Bush,
U.S. First Lady (b. 1925)

REMINDERS

....
....
....
....
....
....

July

18 *Monday*

To prevent the spread of plant viruses, soak the blades of pruning shears in skim milk for 1 minute before moving on to the next plant.

19 *Tuesday*

FULL BUCK MOON

20 *Wednesday*

Today is lucky for those born under the sign of Cancer.

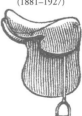

21 *Thursday*

Saddle your dreams before you ride 'em.

–Mary Webb, English writer
(1881–1927)

| JULY • 2016 | | | | | | | AUGUST • 2016 | | | | | |
S	M	T	W	T	F	S	S	M	T	W	T	F	S
					1	2		1	2	3	4	5	6
3	4	5	6	7	8	9	7	8	9	10	11	12	13
10	11	12	13	14	15	16	14	15	16	17	18	19	20
17	18	19	20	21	22	23	21	22	23	24	25	26	27
24	25	26	27	28	29	30	28	29	30	31			
31													

Farm Funnies

Friday 22

Q: What is a sheep's favorite game?

A: Baaaaaadminton.

Saturday 23

Only male crickets chirp.

Sunday 24

Only female mosquitoes bite.

REMINDERS

....

....

....

....

....

....

July

25 Monday

Pioneer Day,
observed (Utah)

Legend claims that a
town in the middle
of Utah was named
Levan because it spells
"navel" backwards.

26 Tuesday

LAST QUARTER

27 Wednesday

Pluto's 16.7 million
square kilometers
of surface could fit
inside Russia.

28 Thursday

*You know you are
getting old when
the candles cost more
than the cake.*

–Bob Hope,
American comedian
(1903–2003)

JULY • 2016	AUGUST • 2016

S	M	T	W	T	F	S
					1	2
3	4	5	6	7	8	9
10	11	12	13	14	15	16
17	18	19	20	21	22	23
24	25	26	27	28	29	30
31						

S	M	T	W	T	F	S
	1	2	3	4	5	6
7	8	9	10	11	12	13
14	15	16	17	18	19	20
21	22	23	24	25	26	27
28	29	30	31			

Friday **29**

When boiling cabbage, drop walnuts (shell on) into the water— they will absorb the odor. Remove them before serving.

Saturday **30**

Have a Popsicle; The climate's tropsicle!
–The Old Farmer's Almanac, 1994

Sunday **31**

In 2013, a 'Carolina Reaper' hot pepper was measured at a scorching 2.2 million Scoville heat units.

REMINDERS

Shakespeare's Seasons

O, how shall summer's honey breath hold out

Against the wreckful siege of battering days,

When rocks impregnable are not so stout,

Nor gates of steel so strong, but Time decays?

—*Sonnet 65*

Moon Probe

How big is our Moon compared to others in our solar system?

As moons go, ours is a big one: It's larger than Pluto and a quarter the size of Earth. But it's only the fifth largest of the 173 known moons in the solar system. The largest is Jupiter's Ganymede, followed by Saturn's Titan, Jupiter's Callisto, and Jupiter's Io.

FULL STURGEON MOON
August 18

Calendar Oddities

Lammas Day: August 1

Derived from an Old English word meaning "loaf mass," this day marked the beginning of the harvest. Loaves of bread baked from the first-ripened grain were brought to church to be consecrated. In Scotland, Lammastide fairs became famous as the time when trial marriages, called handfasting, could be made. They often lasted for a year and a day, after which the couple could separate or be married permanently.

If the first week in August is unusually warm, the winter will be white and long.

125 Years Ago

August 1891

If pears are expected large enough to exhibit at the county fair, the work of thinning must be entered upon with courage and a fixed determination to pick off at least two-thirds of the crop on every full-bearing tree.

—*The Old Farmer's Almanac*

Folklore from Our Ancestors

HOW TO CURE BALDNESS

- Rub the bald spot with cow manure.
- Oil the affected area with the venom of a viper caught at the full Moon.
- Rub the spot daily with axle grease and cod liver oil.
- Cover the bald spot with bear fat.
- Spread cream on the area and let a cat lick it off.

August

1 Monday

Colorado Day

Civic Holiday (Canada)

August brings the sheaves of corn, Then the harvest home is borne.

–Sara Coleridge, English poet (1802–52)

2 Tuesday

NEW MOON

3 Wednesday

Scientists estimate that a single ragweed plant can release 1 billion grains of pollen over the course of a season.

4 Thursday

Seaweed is an excellent fertilizer for citrus trees and roses.

AUGUST • 2016							SEPTEMBER • 2016					
S	M	T	W	T	F	S	S	M	T	W	T	F	S
	1	2	3	4	5	6					1	2	3
7	8	9	10	11	12	13	4	5	6	7	8	9	10
14	15	16	17	18	19	20	11	12	13	14	15	16	17
21	22	23	24	25	26	27	18	19	20	21	22	23	24
28	29	30	31				25	26	27	28	29	30	

Friday

5

When a dog or cat eats grass in the morning, it will rain before nightfall.

Saturday

6

Weeding and table tennis both burn approximately 0.033 of a calorie per minute per pound of body weight.

Sunday

7

Lettuce is like conversation: It must be fresh and crisp, so sparkling that you scarcely notice the bitter in it.

–Charles Dudley Warner, American editor (1829–1900)

REMINDERS

....
....
....
....
....
....

Complement this calendar with daily weather and Almanac wit and wisdom at Almanac.com.

August

8 *Monday*

Today is Sneak Some Zucchini Onto Your Neighbor's Porch Day.

9 *Tuesday*

Don't sweat the petty things and don't pet the sweaty things.

–George Carlin, American comedian (1937–2008)

10 *Wednesday*

FIRST QUARTER

11 *Thursday*

In the language of fruit and vegetables, endive means frugality.

AUGUST • 2016	SEPTEMBER • 2016

AUGUST • 2016

S	M	T	W	T	F	S
	1	2	3	4	5	6
7	8	9	10	11	12	13
14	15	16	17	18	19	20
21	22	23	24	25	26	27
28	29	30	31			

SEPTEMBER • 2016

S	M	T	W	T	F	S
				1	2	3
4	5	6	7	8	9	10
11	12	13	14	15	16	17
18	19	20	21	22	23	24
25	26	27	28	29	30	

Friday 12

It is good luck to throw back
the first fish you catch.

Saturday 13

Aggregating
anemones have the
ability to rapidly
clone themselves.

Sunday 14

A dot placed at the end
of your handwritten
signature shows
that you are guarded.

REMINDERS

....

....

....

....

....

....

August

15 Monday

Discovery Day (Y.T.)

If the Sun goes
pale to bed,
'Twill rain tomorrow,
it is said.

16 Tuesday

Bennington Battle Day (Vt.)

Vermont produces
about 500,000
gallons of maple
syrup each year.

17 Wednesday

*The fixity of a habit
is generally in
direct proportion to
its absurdity.*

–Marcel Proust, French writer
(1871–1922)

18 Thursday

FULL STURGEON MOON

AUGUST • 2016							SEPTEMBER • 2016					
S	M	T	W	T	F	S	S	M	T	W	T	F	S
	1	2	3	4	5	6					1	2	3
7	8	9	10	11	12	13	4	5	6	7	8	9	10
14	15	16	17	18	19	20	11	12	13	14	15	16	17
21	22	23	24	25	26	27	18	19	20	21	22	23	24
28	29	30	31				25	26	27	28	29	30	

Friday 19

National Aviation Day

NASA's vehicle assembly building is so big that it has its own weather: If the air-conditioning is off on humid days, mist can form inside.

Saturday 20

To go fishing is the chance to wash one's soul with pure air.

–Herbert Hoover,
31st U.S. president
(1874–1964)

Sunday 21

'Tis the farmer's care that makes the field bear.

–American proverb

REMINDERS

....
....
....
....
....

August

22 *Monday*

Farm Funnies

Q: Why did the turkey
cross the road twice?

A: To prove he
wasn't chicken.

23 *Tuesday*

Today is lucky for those
born under the sign of Leo.

24 *Wednesday*

LAST QUARTER

25 *Thursday*

A summer's day
palindrome: It's
"too hot to hoot."

AUGUST • 2016							SEPTEMBER • 2016						
S	M	T	W	T	F	S	S	M	T	W	T	F	S
	1	2	3	4	5	6					1	2	3
7	8	9	10	11	12	13	4	5	6	7	8	9	10
14	15	16	17	18	19	20	11	12	13	14	15	16	17
21	22	23	24	25	26	27	18	19	20	21	22	23	24
28	29	30	31				25	26	27	28	29	30	

Friday 26

Women's Equality Day

A woman's mind is cleaner than a man's. She changes it more often.

–Oliver Herford, American writer
(1863–1935)

Saturday 27

Bubbles floating on the surface of your tea suggest that money is in store.

Sunday 28

An egg white will help to remove chewing gum from hair.

REMINDERS

....
....
....
....
....
....

August ❧ September

29 *Monday*

A questioning man is
halfway to being wise.
—*Irish proverb*

30 *Tuesday*

Having trouble
getting to sleep?
Try to yawn—
then yawn again.
Yawning makes
you feel sleepy.

31 *Wednesday*

The dews of April
and May
Make August and
September gay.

1 *Thursday*

NEW MOON

AUGUST • 2016							SEPTEMBER • 2016					
S	M	T	W	T	F	S	S	M	T	W	T	F	S
	1	2	3	4	5	6					1	2	3
7	8	9	10	11	12	13	4	5	6	7	8	9	10
14	15	16	17	18	19	20	11	12	13	14	15	16	17
21	22	23	24	25	26	27	18	19	20	21	22	23	24
28	29	30	31				25	26	27	28	29	30	

Friday 2

The 2017 Old Farmer's Almanac 225th anniversary edition is available now.

Saturday 3

Warm September brings the fruit, Sportsmen then begin to shoot.

–Sara Coleridge, English poet (1802–52)

Sunday 4

Store winter squashes and pumpkins under a bed in an unheated room.

REMINDERS

....
....
....
....
....
....

Shakespeare's Seasons

For his bounty, there was no winter in't; an autumn 'twas that grew the more by reaping.

—Antony and Cleopatra

Moon Probe

Why can we sometimes see a part of the Moon that is not lit by the Sun?

Leonardo da Vinci was the first to figure out the answer: It's earthshine. This is sunlight that bounces off Earth, redirects to the Moon, and then reflects back to us, so that we see dimly lit areas of the Moon that are not directly illuminated by the Sun. Earthshine is especially noticeable when the Moon appears as a crescent. On the Moon, full Earth appears nearly four times larger than the Sun appears to us, and it shines 50 times brighter than a full Moon.

FULL HARVEST MOON
September 16

Calendar Oddities

Harvest Home: September 22

In Europe, the conclusion of the harvest was marked by festivals of feasting and thanksgiving. It was also a time to hold elections, pay workers, and collect rents. These events usually took place around the autumnal equinox. In the United States, the Pennsylvania Dutch and others have kept the tradition alive.

On Michaelmas Day [Sept. 29], the devil puts his foot on the blackberries.

125 Years Ago

September 1891

Don't go to the agricultural fair and say that you could have brought better produce than any on exhibition. If true, it would show a want of public spirit and a lack of interest in the societies that are doing so much to improve the financial condition of the farmer.

—The Old Farmer's Almanac

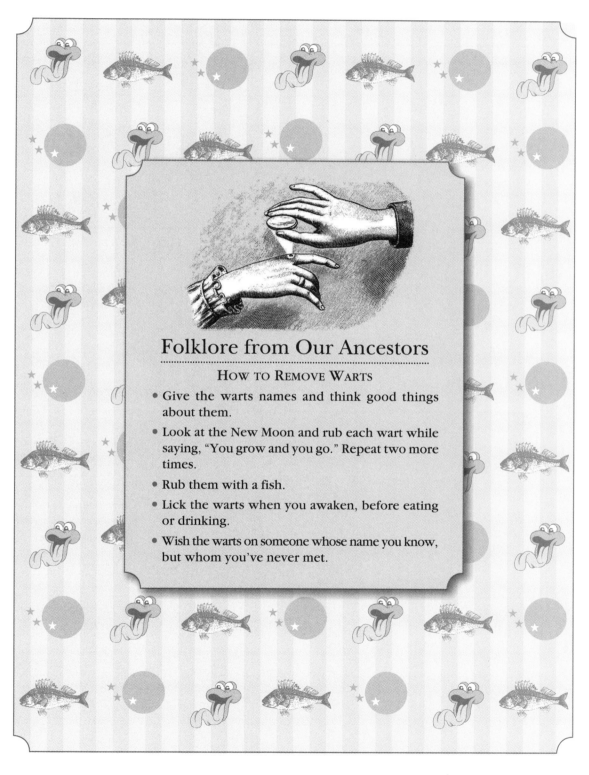

Folklore from Our Ancestors

HOW TO REMOVE WARTS

- Give the warts names and think good things about them.

- Look at the New Moon and rub each wart while saying, "You grow and you go." Repeat two more times.

- Rub them with a fish.

- Lick the warts when you awaken, before eating or drinking.

- Wish the warts on someone whose name you know, but whom you've never met.

September

5 Monday

Labor Day

Rest is the sweet sauce of labor.
–American proverb

6 Tuesday

A hen turns her egg over about 50 times a day to keep the yolk from sticking to the shell.

7 Wednesday

Describing her first day back in grade school after a long absence, a teacher said, "It was like trying to hold 35 corks under water at the same time."

–Mark Twain, American writer (1835–1910)

8 Thursday

Seed new lawns before the leaves fall.

SEPTEMBER • 2016	OCTOBER • 2016
S M T W T F S	S M T W T F S
1 2 3	1
4 5 6 7 8 9 10	2 3 4 5 6 7 8
11 12 13 14 15 16 17	9 10 11 12 13 14 15
18 19 20 21 22 23 24	16 17 18 19 20 21 22
25 26 27 28 29 30	23 24 25 26 27 28 29
	30 31

Friday 9

FIRST QUARTER

Admission Day (Calif.)

Saturday 10

Today is lucky for those
born under the sign of Virgo.

Sunday 11

Patriot Day

Grandparents Day

*Grandparents sort
of sprinkle stardust
over the lives of
little children.*

–Alex Haley, American writer
(1921–92)

REMINDERS

....
....
....
....
....
....

September

12 Monday

One crossbar for two t's together in handwriting shows that you are an effective planner.

13 Tuesday

Expect good fortune if a black dog follows you home.

14 Wednesday

In the language of fruit and vegetables, fig means longevity.

15 Thursday

Charlie Taft, son of President William Taft (born on this day in 1857), brought a copy of *Treasure Island* to his father's inauguration speech in case he got bored.

SEPTEMBER • 2016							OCTOBER • 2016						
S	M	T	W	T	F	S	S	M	T	W	T	F	S
				1	2	3							1
4	5	6	7	8	9	10	2	3	4	5	6	7	8
11	12	13	14	15	16	17	9	10	11	12	13	14	15
18	19	20	21	22	23	24	16	17	18	19	20	21	22
25	26	27	28	29	30		23	24	25	26	27	28	29
							30	31					

Friday **16**

FULL HARVEST MOON

Constitution Day, traditional

Saturday **17**

*Act well your
part; there all the
honor lies.*

–*The Old Farmer's Almanac,* 1884

Sunday **18**

Fence posts should
be set in the dark of the
Moon (between full and
new) to resist rotting.

R E M I N D E R S

....
....
....
....
....
....

September

19 *Monday*

Zebra fish are biologically similar to people and share 70% of the same genes as humans.

20 *Tuesday*

Farm Funnies

Q: Why did the scarecrow win the Nobel Prize?

A: Because he was out standing in his field.

21 *Wednesday*

International Day of Peace

Peace flourishes when reason rules.

—American proverb

22 *Thursday*

Autumnal Equinox

As the wind and weather at the equinoxes, so will they be for the next 3 months.

SEPTEMBER • 2016						
S	M	T	W	T	F	S
				1	2	3
4	5	6	7	8	9	10
11	12	13	14	15	16	17
18	19	20	21	22	23	24
25	26	27	28	29	30	

OCTOBER • 2016						
S	M	T	W	T	F	S
						1
2	3	4	5	6	7	8
9	10	11	12	13	14	15
16	17	18	19	20	21	22
23	24	25	26	27	28	29
30	31					

Friday **23**

LAST QUARTER

Saturday **24**

To float in water, armadillos gulp air to inflate their stomachs and intestines.

Sunday **25**

Pick brussels sprouts and parsnips once they've been exposed to frost.

REMINDERS

....
....
....
....
....
....

September ✦ October

26 *Monday*

Expect foul weather when your cat snores.

27 *Tuesday*

I base most of my fashion sense on what doesn't itch.

–Gilda Radner,
American comedienne (1946–89)

28 *Wednesday*

In Oregon's Malheur National Forest, there is an underground mushroom that covers 2,385 acres.

29 *Thursday*

For greater success, begin new ventures with the new Moon (tomorrow).

SEPTEMBER • 2016	OCTOBER • 2016
S M T W T F S	S M T W T F S
1 2 3	1
4 5 6 7 8 9 10	2 3 4 5 6 7 8
11 12 13 14 15 16 17	9 10 11 12 13 14 15
18 19 20 21 22 23 24	16 17 18 19 20 21 22
25 26 27 28 29 30	23 24 25 26 27 28 29
	30 31

Friday **30**

NEW MOON

Saturday **1**

Islamic New Year
begins at sundown

**Ideas should be clear and
chocolate thick.**

–Spanish proverb

Sunday **2**

Rosh Hashanah
begins at sundown

**Soak toothbrushes in
mouthwash to
discourage colds.**

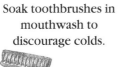

REMINDERS

....
....
....
....
....
....

Shakespeare's Seasons

That time of year thou mayst in me behold

When yellow leaves, or none, or few, do hang

Upon those boughs which shake against the cold,

Bare ruined choirs, where late the sweet birds sang.

—Sonnet 73

Moon Probe

Why is it that the Moon is just the right size to cover the Sun during a total solar eclipse?

Science writer Isaac Asimov once explained, "There is no astronomical reason why the Moon and the Sun should fit so well. It is the sheerest of coincidences." After about 500 million years, there will be no total solar eclipses. The Moon's orbit will have expanded to the point where the Moon appears too small to completely cover the Sun.

FULL HUNTER'S MOON
October 16

Calendar Oddities

St. Luke's Little Summer: October 18

This is a spell of warm weather that occurs on or around the feast day of St. Luke. It is not to be confused with the Indian summer that traditionally occurs in November.

When birds and badgers are fat in October, expect a cold winter.

125 Years Ago

October 1891

There is always a best time to harvest each crop, and it should be the aim of the farmer to find out when it is. To gather a crop too soon, or to let it remain ungathered too long, reduces its value.

—The Old Farmer's Almanac

Folklore from Our Ancestors

HOW TO AVOID DYING PREMATURELY

- Keep cats off the piano keys.
- Don't hang your sweetheart's picture upside down.
- If you see a will-o'-the-wisp while out walking at night, turn your coat inside out.
- Never sleep with your head at the foot of the bed.
- Avoid wearing new clothes to a funeral, especially new shoes.

October

3 *Monday*

Child Health Day

One of the virtues of being very young is that you don't let the facts get in the way of your imagination.

–Samuel Levenson,
American humorist (1911–80)

4 *Tuesday*

When making piecrust, get creative with carving ventilation holes: Try hearts, leaves, or stars.

5 *Wednesday*

If a crab apple tree hangs over the well and blooms out of season, there will be marriage and fertility.

6 *Thursday*

Plant scented tulips, such as 'Apricot Beauty' and 'Generaal de Wet', for a spring display.

OCTOBER • 2016

S	M	T	W	T	F	S
						1
2	3	4	5	6	7	8
9	10	11	12	13	14	15
16	17	18	19	20	21	22
23	24	25	26	27	28	29
30	31					

NOVEMBER • 2016

S	M	T	W	T	F	S
		1	2	3	4	5
6	7	8	9	10	11	12
13	14	15	16	17	18	19
20	21	22	23	24	25	26
27	28	29	30			

Minds are like parachutes— they function only when open.

–attributed to Sir James Dewar, Scottish scientist (1842–1923)

Friday

7

Saturdays are propitious for setting sail.

Saturday

8

Sunday

9

FIRST QUARTER

Leif Eriksson Day

REMINDERS

....
....
....
....
....
....

Complement this calendar with daily weather and Almanac wit and wisdom at Almanac.com.

October

10 Monday

Columbus Day (observed)

Thanksgiving Day (Canada)

Columbus's favorite ship, *Santa Clara,* was owned by Juan Niño—hence its nickname, *Niña.*

11 Tuesday

Yom Kippur begins at sundown

Ease a headache by drinking tomato juice blended with fresh basil.

12 Wednesday

Moles make more molehills during a waxing Moon.

13 Thursday

Fresh October brings the pheasants, Then to gather nuts is pleasant.

–Sara Coleridge, English poet (1802–52)

OCTOBER • 2016

S	M	T	W	T	F	S
						1
2	3	4	5	6	7	8
9	10	11	12	13	14	15
16	17	18	19	20	21	22
23	24	25	26	27	28	29
30	31					

NOVEMBER • 2016

S	M	T	W	T	F	S
		1	2	3	4	5
6	7	8	9	10	11	12
13	14	15	16	17	18	19
20	21	22	23	24	25	26
27	28	29	30			

Handwriting with tall, dominant capital letters shows that you are artistic and imaginative.

Friday 14

In the language of fruit and vegetables, turnip means charity.

Saturday 15

FULL HUNTER'S MOON

Sunday 16

REMINDERS

....
....
....
....
....
....

October

17 *Monday*

Today is lucky for those
born under the sign of Libra.

18 *Tuesday*

Alaska Day

Alaska has more than
40 active volcanoes.

19 *Wednesday*

*I'd rather
take coffee
than compliments
just now.*

–Louisa May Alcott,
American writer (1832–88)

20 *Thursday*

For an auspicious marriage,
the bride and groom
should go home by
a route different from
the one they took to
their nuptials.

OCTOBER • 2016

S M T W T F S
1
2 3 4 5 6 7 8
9 10 11 12 13 14 15
16 17 18 19 20 21 22
23 24 25 26 27 28 29
30 31

NOVEMBER • 2016

S M T W T F S
1 2 3 4 5
6 7 8 9 10 11 12
13 14 15 16 17 18 19
20 21 22 23 24 25 26
27 28 29 30

Friday 21

When cooking with
tomatoes, avoid
using aluminum pans
or utensils.

Saturday 22

LAST QUARTER

Sunday 23

Expect an icy winter
when beavers store short
lengths of aspen and
birch with bark intact.

REMINDERS

....
....
....
....
....
....

October

24 *Monday*

United Nations Day

There is no room for two
feet in one shoe.

—Greek proverb

25 *Tuesday*

Preserve fall leaves
by boiling 1 part
glycerin with 2 parts
water. Soak leaves
and stems overnight
in the solution.

26 *Wednesday*

October breezy,
November wheezy,
December freezy.

27 *Thursday*

At age 42, Theodore
Roosevelt (born
on this day in 1858)
was the youngest
U.S. president.

OCTOBER • 2016

S	M	T	W	T	F	S
						1
2	3	4	5	6	7	8
9	10	11	12	13	14	15
16	17	18	19	20	21	22
23	24	25	26	27	28	29
30	31					

NOVEMBER • 2016

S	M	T	W	T	F	S
		1	2	3	4	5
6	7	8	9	10	11	12
13	14	15	16	17	18	19
20	21	22	23	24	25	26
27	28	29	30			

Friday **28**

Nevada Day

Nevada's state precious gemstone is the black fire opal.

Saturday **29**

Friendship is certainly the finest balm for the pangs of disappointed love.

–Jane Austen, English writer (1775–1817)

Sunday **30**

NEW MOON

REMINDERS

....
....
....
....
....
....

October ❧ November

31 Monday

Halloween

Farm Funnies

Q: What do you call a haunting chicken?

A: A poultry-geist.

1 Tuesday

A black box feels heavier than a white box of equal weight.

2 Wednesday

If you dream of a hedgehog, you'll see an old friend soon.

3 Thursday

Of course I have played outdoor sports. I once played dominoes in an open-air café in Paris.

–Oscar Wilde, Irish writer (1854–1900)

OCTOBER • 2016	NOVEMBER • 2016
S M T W T F S	S M T W T F S
1	1 2 3 4 5
2 3 4 5 6 7 8	6 7 8 9 10 11 12
9 10 11 12 13 14 15	13 14 15 16 17 18 19
16 17 18 19 20 21 22	20 21 22 23 24 25 26
23 24 25 26 27 28 29	27 28 29 30
30 31	

Will Rogers Day (Okla.)

Friday **4**

Oklahoma's state
vegetable is the
watermelon.

Substitute cold milk
for water in your
favorite piecrust
recipe. The result will
be a flaky crust
that browns evenly.

Saturday **5**

Daylight Saving Time ends at 2:00 A.M.

Sunday **6**

*The future ain't what
it used to be.*

–Yogi Berra,
American baseball player (b. 1925)

REMINDERS

....

....

....

....

....

....

Shakespeare's Seasons

Thus sometimes hath the brightest day a cloud;

And after summer evermore succeeds

Barren winter, with his wrathful nipping cold:

So cares and joys abound, as seasons fleet.

—*Henry VI, Part 2*

Moon Probe

Is there water on the Moon?

Yes. There is evidence that water ice exists in deep, permanently shaded craters at both the north and south poles of the Moon. The ice may have come from asteroids, meteorites, and comets that continuously pummel the Moon's surface, or it may have been produced when solar wind interacted with oxygen held in lunar minerals.

FULL BEAVER MOON
November 14

Calendar Oddities

Indian Summer: November 11

Although there are differing dates for Indian summer's occurrence, the Almanac has adhered to the saying, "If All Saints' [November 1] brings out winter, St. Martin's [November 11] brings out Indian summer." In colonial times, some Native Americans in New England believed that the warm spell was caused by winds from their southwestern god, Cautantowwit.

If the geese at Martin's Day [Nov. 11] stand on ice, they will walk in mud at Christmas.

125 Years Ago

November 1891

When the fall work is all finished and the ground frozen, sharpen up the axe and start bright and early for the woods, so that the firewood may be all cut before the snow gets too deep.

—The Old Farmer's Almanac

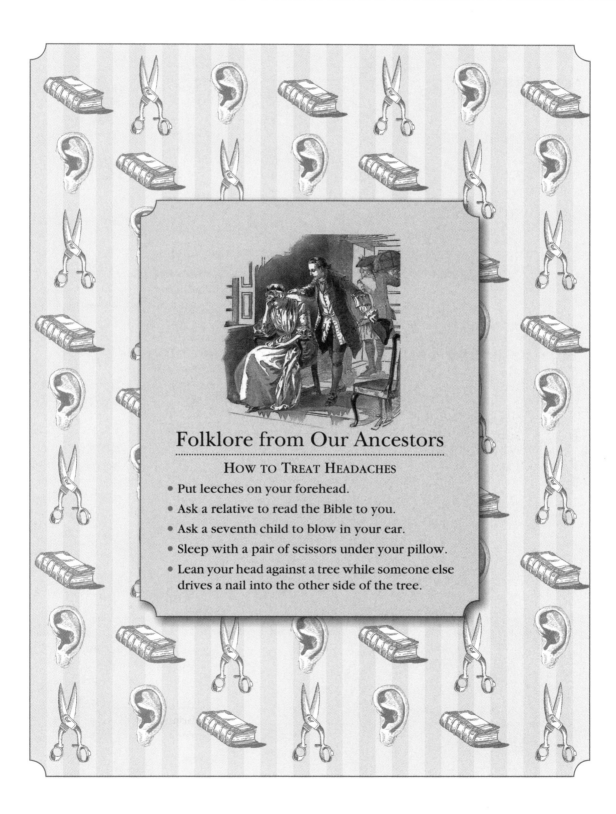

Folklore from Our Ancestors

HOW TO TREAT HEADACHES

- Put leeches on your forehead.
- Ask a relative to read the Bible to you.
- Ask a seventh child to blow in your ear.
- Sleep with a pair of scissors under your pillow.
- Lean your head against a tree while someone else drives a nail into the other side of the tree.

November

7 Monday

FIRST QUARTER

8 Tuesday

Election Day

An election-day palindrome: Rise to vote, sir.

9 Wednesday

Dull November brings the blast, Then the leaves are whirling fast.

–Sara Coleridge, English poet (1802–52)

10 Thursday

Top asparagus plants with compost or manure for fatter spears next year.

NOVEMBER • 2016	DECEMBER • 2016
S M T W T F S	S M T W T F S

NOVEMBER • 2016
S M T W T F S
        1 2 3 4 5
 6 7 8 9 10 11 12
13 14 15 16 17 18 19
20 21 22 23 24 25 26
27 28 29 30

DECEMBER • 2016
S M T W T F S
           1 2 3
 4 5 6 7 8 9 10
11 12 13 14 15 16 17
18 19 20 21 22 23 24
25 26 27 28 29 30 31

Friday **11**

Veterans Day

Remembrance Day (Canada)

*Gratitude is the sign
of noble souls.*

–Aesop, Greek writer
(c. 620 B.C.–c. 560 B.C.)

Saturday **12**

December gets busy;
make appointments for
haircuts now.

Sunday **13**

The full Moon (tomorrow)
is an ideal time to accept a
marriage proposal.

REMINDERS

....
....
....
....
....

November

14 *Monday*

FULL BEAVER MOON

15 *Tuesday*

The thing that impresses me most about America is the way parents obey their children.

–Edward VIII, Duke of Windsor
(1894–1972)

16 *Wednesday*

Today is lucky for those born under the sign of Scorpio.

17 *Thursday*

To make butternut squash easier to cut and peel, pierce the skin in a few places and then microwave the squash for 2 to 3 minutes.

NOVEMBER • 2016

S	M	T	W	T	F	S
		1	2	3	4	5
6	7	8	9	10	11	12
13	14	15	16	17	18	19
20	21	22	23	24	25	26
27	28	29	30			

DECEMBER • 2016

S	M	T	W	T	F	S
				1	2	3
4	5	6	7	8	9	10
11	12	13	14	15	16	17
18	19	20	21	22	23	24
25	26	27	28	29	30	31

Farm Funnies

Friday **18**

Q: Is a duck with two wings better than a duck with one wing?

A: Why, that's a difference of a pinion.

Discovery of Puerto Rico Day

Saturday **19**

A white speck on your little fingernail foretells a new sweetheart.

National Child Day (Canada)

Sunday **20**

The best smell is bread; the best savor, salt; the best love, that of children.

–George Herbert, Welsh-born English poet (1593–1633)

On the road again from Oklahoma

REMINDERS

....
....
....
....
....
....

November

21 Monday

Arriving Home

LAST QUARTER

22 Tuesday

I skate to where the puck is going to be, not where it has been.

—Wayne Gretzky,
Canadian hockey player
(b. 1961)

23 Wednesday

In the language of fruit and vegetables, gooseberry means anticipation.

24 Thursday

Thanksgiving Day

Zachary Taylor (born on this day in 1784) refused to pay the postage due on a letter, not realizing that it told of his presidential nomination.

NOVEMBER • 2016

S	M	T	W	T	F	S
		1	2	3	4	5
6	7	8	9	10	11	12
13	14	15	16	17	18	19
20	21	22	23	24	25	26
27	28	29	30			

DECEMBER • 2016

S	M	T	W	T	F	S
				1	2	3
4	5	6	7	8	9	10
11	12	13	14	15	16	17
18	19	20	21	22	23	24
25	26	27	28	29	30	31

Acadian Day (La.)

Friday **25**

*In all things of
nature, there is
something of the
marvelous.*

–Aristotle, Greek philosopher
(384–322 B.C.)

---

*I prefer the errors
of enthusiasm
to the indifference
of wisdom.*

–Anatole France,
French writer (1844–1924)

Saturday **26**

The last Sunday in the
month indicates the weather
for the next month.

Sunday **27**

REMINDERS

....
....
....
....
....
....

Complement this calendar with daily weather and Almanac wit and wisdom at Almanac.com.

November ❧ December

28 Monday

Handwriting that has irregular letter sizes shows that you are moody and quick-tempered.

29 Tuesday

NEW MOON

30 Wednesday

My most brilliant achievement was my ability to be able to persuade my wife to marry me.

–Sir Winston Churchill, English statesman (1874–1965)

1 Thursday

On Thursday at three, Look out, and you'll see What Friday will be.

NOVEMBER • 2016

S	M	T	W	T	F	S
		1	2	3	4	5
6	7	8	9	10	11	12
13	14	15	16	17	18	19
20	21	22	23	24	25	26
27	28	29	30			

DECEMBER • 2016

S	M	T	W	T	F	S
				1	2	3
4	5	6	7	8	9	10
11	12	13	14	15	16	17
18	19	20	21	22	23	24
25	26	27	28	29	30	31

Friday

2

Having dressed yourself, pay no further attention to your clothes.

–Ladies Indispensable Assistant,
1852

Saturday

3

Mix together black oil sunflower seeds, safflower seeds, and chopped unsalted peanuts for the birds.

Sunday

4

Truths are not uttered from behind masks.

–Greek proverb

REMINDERS

....

....

....

....

....

....

Shakespeare's Seasons

How like a winter hath my absence been

From thee, the pleasure of the fleeting year!

—Sonnet 97

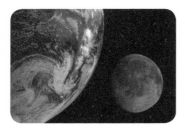

Moon Probe

Will the Moon–Earth relationship ever change?

When the Moon formed 4.5 billion years ago, it was only about 14,000 miles from Earth; it's now more than 280,000 miles out. Currently, the Moon moves away from us by about 1.5 inches each year because of Earth's slowing rotation. But don't worry, it's not going away. Within several billion years, if the aging Sun doesn't get into the picture, the Moon's orbit and Earth's rotation will have stabilized. Earth will have slowed its spin and matched the time that it takes for the Moon to orbit it.

FULL COLD MOON
December 13

Calendar Oddities

Halcyon Days: December

The ancient Greeks and Romans believed that the halcyon, or kingfisher, built its nest at sea and charmed the winds and waves to provide a placid interval in which to raise its young. Thus came to be about 2 weeks of calm weather that often follow the blustery winds of autumn's end.

Thunder during Christmas week means that there will be much snow during the winter.

125 Years Ago

December 1891

Is it not about time to settle up and find out just how much you owe? Don't run up a long bill and then wait to be dunned for it. Have as few bills as possible.

—The Old Farmer's Almanac

Folklore from Our Ancestors

HOW TO CURE HICCUPS

- Pant like a dog.
- Drink nine swallows of water from your grand-father's cup without taking a breath.
- Place the head of a burnt match in your ear.
- Lay a broom on the floor (bristles to the right) and walk around it seven times.
- Wet a piece of red thread with your tongue, stick it to your forehead, and then look at it.

December

5 Monday

Always enter a new
home with a loaf of bread
and new broom.

6 Tuesday

*Chill December
brings the sleet,
Blazing fire, and
Christmas treat.*

–Sara Coleridge,
English poet (1802–52)

7 Wednesday

FIRST QUARTER

National Pearl Harbor
Remembrance Day

8 Thursday

The study of proverbs
is called paremiology.

DECEMBER • 2016	JANUARY • 2017
S M T W T F S	S M T W T F S
1 2 3	1 2 3 4 5 6 7
4 5 6 7 8 9 10	8 9 10 11 12 13 14
11 12 13 14 15 16 17	15 16 17 18 19 20 21
18 19 20 21 22 23 24	22 23 24 25 26 27 28
25 26 27 28 29 30 31	29 30 31

Friday 9

*Indecision may
or may not
be my problem.*
–Jimmy Buffett,
American musician (b. 1946)

Saturday 10

For an "old cough,"
Native Americans
recommended
blueberry juice or
blueberry syrup.

Sunday 11

*Fire up the stove,
please,
Then cut down your
Christmas trees.*
–*The Old Farmer's Almanac*, 1982

REMINDERS

....
....
....
....
....
....

December

12 *Monday*

Farm Funnies

Q: How does the
farmer count his cows?

A: He uses a
cow-culator.

13 *Tuesday*

FULL COLD MOON

14 *Wednesday*

An extra plate at table set,
A hungry guest
you soon will get.

15 *Thursday*

Bill of Rights Day

James Madison penned
the Bill of Rights.

DECEMBER • 2016							JANUARY • 2017						
S	M	T	W	T	F	S	S	M	T	W	T	F	S
				1	2	3	1	2	3	4	5	6	7
4	5	6	7	8	9	10	8	9	10	11	12	13	14
11	12	13	14	15	16	17	15	16	17	18	19	20	21
18	19	20	21	22	23	24	22	23	24	25	26	27	28
25	26	27	28	29	30	31	29	30	31				

Friday 16

*Of all the trees
that are in the wood,
the holly bears
the crown.*

–"The Holly and the Ivy,"
traditional English carol

Saturday 17

Wright Brothers Day

Today is lucky for
those born under the sign
of Sagittarius.

Sunday 18

*Quote me as saying
I was misquoted.*

–Groucho Marx, American actor
(1890–1977)

REMINDERS

....

....

....

....

....

....

Complement this calendar with daily weather and Almanac wit and wisdom at Almanac.com.

December

19 *Monday*

In the language of fruit and vegetables, pomegranate means foolishness.

20 *Tuesday*

LAST QUARTER

21 *Wednesday*

Winter Solstice

Winter is on my head, but eternal spring is in my heart.

–Victor Hugo, French writer (1802–85)

22 *Thursday*

Before cooking for the holidays, remove kitchen clutter to make room for the preparations.

DECEMBER • 2016	JANUARY • 2017
S M T W T F S	S M T W T F S
1 2 3	1 2 3 4 5 6 7
4 5 6 7 8 9 10	8 9 10 11 12 13 14
11 12 13 14 15 16 17	15 16 17 18 19 20 21
18 19 20 21 22 23 24	22 23 24 25 26 27 28
25 26 27 28 29 30 31	29 30 31

Friday **23**

Handwriting with
capital letters that
slant down to the right
shows that you are
diplomatic.

Saturday **24**

Chanukah begins at sundown

***Content lodges
oftener in cottages
than palaces.***

–Thomas Fuller,
English clergyman (1608–61)

Sunday **25**

𝕮𝖍𝖗𝖎𝖘𝖙𝖒𝖆𝖘 𝕯𝖆𝖞

Stand under the
mistletoe: A passionate
kiss burns the calories
of one potato chip.

REMINDERS

....

....

....

....

....

December 2016 ❧ January 2017

26 *Monday*

Boxing Day (Canada)

First day of Kwanzaa

A good hope is better than a bad possession.
–Spanish proverb

27 *Tuesday*

In the 1600s, American colonists called apples "winter bananas."

28 *Wednesday*

In memory, everything seems to happen to music.
–Tennessee Williams, American writer (1911–83)

29 *Thursday*

NEW MOON

DECEMBER • 2016	JANUARY • 2017
S M T W T F S	S M T W T F S
1 2 3	1 2 3 4 5 6 7
4 5 6 7 8 9 10	8 9 10 11 12 13 14
11 12 13 14 15 16 17	15 16 17 18 19 20 21
18 19 20 21 22 23 24	22 23 24 25 26 27 28
25 26 27 28 29 30 31	29 30 31

Friday 30

The second day of the new Moon is propitious for buying or selling.

Saturday 31

On New Year's Eve in Romania, people dress as bears and visit homes to scare off troublesome spirits.

Sunday 1

New Year's Day

If you receive a coin today and do not spend it, you will have money all year long.

REMINDERS

....
....
....
....
....
....

2017 Advance Planner

bold = *U.S. and/or Canadian national holidays*

JANUARY • 2017

S	M	T	W	T	F	S
1	2	3	4	5	6	7
8	9	10	11	12	13	14
15	**16**	17	18	19	20	21
22	23	24	25	26	27	28
29	30	31				

FEBRUARY • 2017

S	M	T	W	T	F	S
			1	2	3	4
5	6	7	8	9	10	11
12	13	14	15	16	17	18
19	**20**	21	22	23	24	25
26	27	28				

MARCH • 2017

S	M	T	W	T	F	S
			1	2	3	4
5	6	7	8	9	10	11
12	13	14	15	16	17	18
19	20	21	22	23	24	25
26	27	28	29	30	31	

APRIL • 2017

S	M	T	W	T	F	S
						1
2	3	4	5	6	7	8
9	10	11	12	13	**14**	15
16	**17**	18	19	20	21	22
23	24	25	26	27	28	29
30						

MAY • 2017

S	M	T	W	T	F	S
	1	2	3	4	5	6
7	8	9	10	11	12	13
14	15	16	17	18	19	20
21	**22**	23	24	25	26	27
28	**29**	30	31			

JUNE • 2017

S	M	T	W	T	F	S
				1	2	3
4	5	6	7	8	9	10
11	12	13	14	15	16	17
18	19	20	21	22	23	24
25	26	27	28	29	30	

JULY • 2017

S	M	T	W	T	F	S
						1
2	3	**4**	5	6	7	8
9	10	11	12	13	14	15
16	17	18	19	20	21	22
23	24	25	26	27	28	29
30	31					

AUGUST • 2017

S	M	T	W	T	F	S
		1	2	3	4	5
6	7	8	9	10	11	12
13	14	15	16	17	18	19
20	21	22	23	24	25	26
27	28	29	30	31		

SEPTEMBER • 2017

S	M	T	W	T	F	S
					1	2
3	**4**	5	6	7	8	9
10	11	12	13	14	15	16
17	18	19	20	21	22	23
24	25	26	27	28	29	30

OCTOBER • 2017

S	M	T	W	T	F	S
1	2	3	4	5	6	7
8	**9**	10	11	12	13	14
15	16	17	18	19	20	21
22	23	24	25	26	27	28
29	30	31				

NOVEMBER • 2017

S	M	T	W	T	F	S
			1	2	3	4
5	6	7	8	9	10	**11**
12	13	14	15	16	17	18
19	20	21	22	**23**	24	25
26	27	28	29	30		

DECEMBER • 2017

S	M	T	W	T	F	S
					1	2
3	4	5	6	7	8	9
10	11	12	13	14	15	16
17	18	19	20	21	22	23
24	**25**	**26**	27	28	29	30
31						

2018 Advance Planner

bold = *U.S. and/or Canadian national holidays*

JANUARY • 2018

S	M	T	W	T	F	S
	1	2	3	4	5	6
7	8	9	10	11	12	13
14	**15**	16	17	18	19	20
21	22	23	24	25	26	27
28	29	30	31			

FEBRUARY • 2018

S	M	T	W	T	F	S
				1	2	3
4	5	6	7	8	9	10
11	12	13	14	15	16	17
18	**19**	20	21	22	23	24
25	26	27	28			

MARCH • 2018

S	M	T	W	T	F	S
				1	2	3
4	5	6	7	8	9	10
11	12	13	14	15	16	17
18	19	20	21	22	23	24
25	26	27	28	29	**30**	31

APRIL • 2018

S	M	T	W	T	F	S
1	**2**	3	4	5	6	7
8	9	10	11	12	13	14
15	16	17	18	19	20	21
22	23	24	25	26	27	28
29	30					

MAY • 2018

S	M	T	W	T	F	S
		1	2	3	4	5
6	7	8	9	10	11	12
13	14	15	16	17	18	19
20	**21**	22	23	24	25	26
27	**28**	29	30	31		

JUNE • 2018

S	M	T	W	T	F	S
					1	2
3	4	5	6	7	8	9
10	11	12	13	14	15	16
17	18	19	20	21	22	23
24	25	26	27	28	29	30

JULY • 2018

S	M	T	W	T	F	S
1	2	3	**4**	5	6	7
8	9	10	11	12	13	14
15	16	17	18	19	20	21
22	23	24	25	26	27	28
29	30	31				

AUGUST • 2018

S	M	T	W	T	F	S
			1	2	3	4
5	6	7	8	9	10	11
12	13	14	15	16	17	18
19	20	21	22	23	24	25
26	27	28	29	30	31	

SEPTEMBER • 2018

S	M	T	W	T	F	S
						1
2	**3**	4	5	6	7	8
9	10	11	12	13	14	15
16	17	18	19	20	21	22
23	24	25	26	27	28	29
30						

OCTOBER • 2018

S	M	T	W	T	F	S
	1	2	3	4	5	6
7	**8**	9	10	11	12	13
14	15	16	17	18	19	20
21	22	23	24	25	26	27
28	29	30	31			

NOVEMBER • 2018

S	M	T	W	T	F	S
				1	2	3
4	5	6	7	8	9	10
11	12	13	14	15	16	17
18	19	20	21	**22**	23	24
25	26	27	28	29	30	

DECEMBER • 2018

S	M	T	W	T	F	S
						1
2	3	4	5	6	7	8
9	10	11	12	13	14	15
16	17	18	19	20	21	22
23	24	**25**	**26**	27	28	29
30	31					

Planning a trip? See the Long-Range Weather Forecast at Almanac.com/Weather.

Birthdays and Anniversaries

Name	Birthday	Anniversary

Addresses and Phone Numbers

Name _____ Home _____

Address _____ Work _____

_____ Cell _____

Email _____ Fax _____

Web site _____

Name _____ Home _____

Address _____ Work _____

_____ Cell _____

Email _____ Fax _____

Web site _____

Name _____ Home _____

Address _____ Work _____

_____ Cell _____

Email _____ Fax _____

Web site _____

Name _____ Home _____

Address _____ Work _____

_____ Cell _____

Email _____ Fax _____

Web site _____

Name _____ Home _____

Address _____ Work _____

_____ Cell _____

Email _____ Fax _____

Web site _____

Name _____ Home _____

Address _____ Work _____

_____ Cell _____

Email _____ Fax _____

Web site _____

Emergency Contacts

In case of emergency, notify:

Name _____ Relationship _____

Address _____

_____

Phone _____ Email _____

Police department _____

Fire department _____

Ambulance _____

Hospital _____

Poison control _____

Physician _____

Dentist _____

Veterinarian _____

Pharmacy _____

Clergy _____

Electric company _____

Electrician _____

Plumber _____

Auto mechanic _____

Baby-sitter _____

School(s) _____

Insurance:

    Auto _____

    Homeowner's _____

    Health _____

    Dental _____

Other _____

_____

_____

_____

_____

_____